TARKOVSKY'S HORSES
AND OTHER POEMS

Pia Tafdrup was born in 1952 in Copenhagen. She has published over 20 books in Danish since her first collection appeared in 1981, and her work has been translated into many languages. Her fourth collection, *Spring Tide*, was published in English by Forest in 1989. In 1991 she published a celebrated statement of her poetics, *Walking Over Water*. She received the 1999 Nordic Council Literature Prize – Scandinavia's most prestigious literary award – for *Queen's Gate*, which was published in David McDuff's English translation by Bloodaxe Books in 2001. Also in 2001, she was appointed a Knight of the Order of Dannebrog, and in 2006 she received the Nordic Prize from the Swedish Academy. In 2009 she won the international Jan Smrek Prize (awarded to non-Slovak, foreign poets) for her poetry.

Her latest work translated into English is *Tarkovsky's Horses and other poems* (Bloodaxe Books, 2010), a Poetry Book Society Recommended Translation, combining *The Whales in Paris* (2002) and *Tarkovsky's Horses* (2006), both published in Denmark by Gyldendal.

Pia Tafdrup's website: www.tafdrup.com

PIA TAFDRUP

TARKOVSKY'S HORSES
AND OTHER POEMS

TRANSLATED BY
DAVID McDUFF

BLOODAXE BOOKS

ISBN: 978 1 85224 837 6

First published 2010 by
Bloodaxe Books Ltd,
Highgreen,
Tarset,
Northumberland NE48 1RP.

www.bloodaxebooks.com
For further information about Bloodaxe titles
please visit our website or write to
the above address for a catalogue.

Supported by
**ARTS COUNCIL
ENGLAND**

ACKNOWLEDGEMENTS
This book is published with the assistance of grants for
translation costs from Kunstrådet, the Danish Arts Council's
Committee for Literature, and from Arts Council England's
Grants for the arts scheme funded by the National Lottery.

LOTTERY FUNDED

Cover design: Neil Astley & Pamela Robertson-Pearce.

Printed in Great Britain by
Bell & Bain Limited, Glasgow, Scotland.

CONTENTS

TARKOVSKY'S HORSES (2006)

OUTRO

THE WHALES IN PARIS

I

No platinum measure for time

Kernel

I was a night in August, on the other side of the planets' ice,
I was a hand that gripped and held fast,
I was an avalanche, a blood-black wall on fire,
I was a strident passage in my mother's heart,
where she had to decide
                    if life was worth living,
I was my father's lust, I was forgiveness,
I was the pulse in the earth, the deepest veins,
I was the dew in the grass one raw, cold morning,
I was flower and nectar scent,
I was a dripping sweetish taste
of the apple with bitter carnelian-red peel,
                              − a kernel,
that rode on the water without sinking
and was washed ashore on a north-facing coast
on the fifty-sixth parallel,
I was the hidden, found by a beam of light,
seen by an angel's eye —
an eye that thought itself lost,
where the shore was salt-white, the sand light as ash,
and the beech-wood forced steep slopes
to reflect themselves in the water,
                         echo on echo...
I was a raging fever in the blood,
I was a membrane that burst, the birds that flew,
I was the murmur in the room beneath the treetops' cupola,
a whirring of sounds that led weightlessly in
where paths are erased,
                and there is no way back,
into the magnetic field of the hidden, into the zone of sucking darkness,
from which all the alphabet's letters spring
− out into the light,
                out into the silence to strike root
                                    in endless present,
where the shadows dwell, and do not assimilate.

Evening Walk in Fælledparken

Pretty, pretty sky, sun
standing behind treetops black as entrails.
Why days when I savour
sound of steel on stone in this
gentle pink light, in this
wind that warms the heart, even though
autumn is running across
the path and the first dry
leaves are rustling through the grass
hurriedly, the way I chain-read
certain never-written letters
merely seduced by fire-fall's desires...
Sun full of promise, that goes in
just because I've arrived too late,
as all too often... Light, light
breeze that makes branches
sway and vibrate gently
in fine, Aeolian patterns,
or be transformed into a
sourish poison placed inside the word,
but hardly lifts fu-
tile days and titanically
heavy thoughts or knows
their flight-path out of the mind...
The year's first stabs of cold
rise naked from the grass's mist,
blend themselves with mild evenings.
Those that are ducks now, dive,
catch, for in a year's time other
broods of young ones will sleeplessly draw
nourishment at this same place in the lake...
Good, good smell of soil,
that makes the dog dance
with a stick in his mouth, until
the dust whirls up, and I
in clouds of it am suddenly invaded
by joy at this day
surviving the light, which so

bluish swiftly vanishes in
between track and tree-trunks, where only
dreams tendril-like flame
aloft and find their star-
height at the wrong address.

Icebreaker Made of Feathers

A thorny night,
a naked copse of darkness.
My sleep crackles gently like the first thin ice
drawn sharply over the lakes.
The autumn's rasping frost-raw odours slam into the room
from an open window that looks north,
                    short-circuit
with roses' spiced scent of a summer's deep, vertiginous dream.
I pluck from the darkness —
wrapped in stabbing silence
I start up after only an hour's dry stinging sleep,
                    afflicted
by jets of poison that rage in my blood,
work of split tongues.
There will hardly be another earth,
and I would have liked to dance here...
An eyelid quivers, a shoulder hurts,
the way is blocked by something I can't make out
in midnight's misty moonlight.
But the swans lift their breasts,
               they break
the fragilely cast crusts of ice on the lakes
with a long-extended creaking of light.
On the path an aftershock spreads,
a chord stroke
on an instrument invisible and rarely used,
depositing glacially multiplying rows of notes,
                    transparent hurryings,
                        from cut to scar —
insight's expanding and constantly vibrating chaos.
An indomitable fragrance spreads
from the white roses that have drunk infinitely of the morning cold.
I swim further out:
          As long as the air carries,
               the last word is not spoken.

II

Three replies to Derrida

What Day, What Hour?

Whose lips?
Someone's lips, a hurried tongue
inside in the shadow and the pathology
or out in the sun,
out in the sun and inside in the genitals,
while the light multiplies itself by itself,
like the breathing.
From upright phase
backwards through arcades of time
to crawling, lying...
No words in the darkness,
because we can't see anything
closed in
        behind lowered eyelids.
A ground never trodden before,
a place to hide
in order to be found
– and opened
by a tongue-tip, by lips,
other lips,
turn round and notice
new lips,
        floating fire,
circles drawn inside circles,
                        dripping fire.
Inhale the slow light —
are turned, sunned, blessed
and give
        sick with love
death
a chance.

What Hour, What Minute?

An offence in life is sometimes punished
by death
– poison – gas – electric chair – firing squad – or hanging —
but what is death,
when it doesn't come as punishment?
It can hardly be a reward?
Condemned to die
are we
– even without punishment.
Or is death
in spite of everything a gift,
as otherwise we would have lived too long?
That would be a punishment!
For ourselves, and for others.
It is hard to see death
as a gift,
when I want to throw away the piece of paper
with the name and address of a friend,
who is death,
because I must remind myself
not to send any more letters, not call any more,
but probably not give up having conversations in dreams...
Shall I hide the frayed scrap of paper
or remember its contents?
It is quiet
in the shadow...
I evacuate the address he wrote for me
– but why?
Because the sky with rising glow
shines red as Herod now —
or because a woodpecker
wanders out on a branch with its feet up
and head down,
          but its gaze
                    along the morning sky of the abyss.

What Minute, What Second?

Neon-green, the night is lit by an exit sign
on the first floor of the building opposite.
There is no accessible exit there for me,
as I don't live in the house,
but if I could let the sign show the way and then leave the house,
I could go
      and follow my own trace back in time,
my feet could dream their way back
through cities, where in the misty greyness
I mixed up the names of streets,
I could go and go
          until seasons moved backwards,
as easily as the clock's hands can be put back,
walk so far
      that time was rewound to
where I could go back to the exact moment
when I first realised: Death
        meant the end —
which again meant consciousness of consciousness's ending.
If I could go down the staircase in that other house,
where one senses that the door is ajar,
and out to the street, all the way back,
          backwards out
of years' labyrinthine tortuous passages
in order to grasp when it dawned on me
what 'till death us do part' meant,
         the transitional moment —
when between systole and diastole
I was determined in my unicity,
        the moment of trembling
which at one stroke set me outside and viewed
life as different from before...
But I have temporarily moved into rooms
where nothing belongs to me,
or where I do not yet recognise the smell of myself
in order once again to be reminded
that my life
is not lived in some alien house,
        but in myself,

where a crackling is accumulated,
as winter stars grow strong.
My traces have been erased —
from this place I can only go to meet time.
Something calls,
        otherwise I would not be
                here,
where the countdown continues uninterrupted.

III

Mutual amputation

Catching Fire

A white blossoming fear, foam seethes
and breaks to nothing,
                    drops burn —
but it is not magic, not alchemy
or domino game of stars.
It is liquid,
        a clear fluid, that fastens on
any skin at all,
                    light, dark or wrong...
An angel flaps its wings
in order to tear itself free from the railings
around the playground,
                    which tomorrow is the world's arena.
There children spray petrol
in a sudden flicker of light.
There children drench a springtime
one pouring light green day, where sparrows
chirrup tropically in the hedge.
There they are setting fire to a playmate,
                            shouting for help,
as flames with a breath
                    leap black-tongued up,
as the skin melts,
as body and shadow are one
and can no longer be separated —
as the silence disfigured screams in several languages
as the child is embalmed alive in shock and raincoat.

Without Mandolin

'Abstract means when you don't recognise something' —
says the woman at the museum to the children on the floor.
The group follows her finger
from 'Man with Guitar' to 'Man with Mandolin'.
On the contrary he is very concrete
                              and not painted by Picasso,
the man who has keeled over on the pavement
and grown together with a plane-tree in bud,
which young folk rush past along the river
in cars paid for by bad conscience of rich fathers,
not heading anywhere in particular, perhaps
to a concert this evening
                        – without mandolin.
They dart past the man, who outcast by himself,
by others,
or casting out the city,
sleeps motionless in a dust-brown coat
with his head on the kerb,
while hungry pigeons peck at his bread... Death
also passes one windless afternoon,
where sunlight hurries between the branches of the tree.
Fire flows in his breast,
                        drags a confusion of flight-tracks.
What is that runs to meet the river,
as the water changes from dark to gold,
                              a glittering wound?
The cold sucks blackly from the earth,
the city closes round the man,
a crooked, coagulated figure no one recognises,
something sealed and alien,
                        which they all, in spite of his open face,
continue to pass by in an arc —
and thus make abstract.

Mirroring

A wall of right-angled silence I have raised,
before it you stand listening for hellish hours.
What's happening on the other side? – You hear
nothing, fill the darkness with ice-blind calling,
you ask but receive no answer —
rummage in pockets, look at letters,
seek
what you want to find, and therefore find:
On the other side the soul is growing strong.
Here it's not quiet at all, here there is love and talk
                                        to another.
The beginning's flames of multiplicity
sluice through the breast.
The sparrows sing early, but not for you,
                                it's for us,
who seek shelter in a dream
embracing each other in our thoughts all day and night.
– There must be silence
to preserve the mystery, I say to you.
You move a mountain, realise
that our two parallel lives don't meet
at any point,
while what we have lost points towards us
from nearly all directions.
Is time a star
ground to dust
or dust
gathered to a star?
You send me away, so I can think about
                                my free life,
so tormented that I can't hear the birds,
which now are singing for you,
                                beloved.

A wall of right-angled silence you have raised,
Before it I stand listening for hellish hours.
What's happening on the other side? – I hear
nothing, fill the darkness with ice-blind calling,
I ask but get no answer —

rummage in pockets, look at letters,
seek
what I want to find, and therefore find:
On the other side the soul is growing strong.
There it's not quiet at all, there is love and talk
                                        to another.
The beginning's flames of multiplicity
will sluice through the breast.
The sparrows sing early, but not for me,
                              it's for the two of you,
who seek shelter in a dream
embracing each other in your thoughts all day round.
– There must be silence
to preserve the mystery, you say to me.
I move a mountain, realise
that our two parallel lives don't meet
at any point,
while what we have lost points towards us
from nearly all directions.
Is time a star
ground to dust
or dust
gathered to a star?
I send you away, so you can think about
                              your free life,
so tormented that you won't be able to hear the birds,
which now are singing for me,
                        whom you love.

Moon-grey Echo

Blind ambulance wailing, emergency admission of a motionless body,
a heart sleeps its incipient stone sleep —
you don't hear shouts,
                    slaps in the face you don't heed,
day and night are already one.
In through the vestibule, through lit ravines at a fevered pace,
through tunnel depths, past soundless niches,
coats in panic-white movements,
                    in and out and in.
Doors swing open and shut
                    and back again
– into the midst of the labyrinth, into
a room where chlorine-blinding light is switched on,
and instruments clink metallically pure, up on to the couch
where your earth-smelling, heavy body is rolled about
and emptied of poison.
Further, in to the beast in the cave,
the warm beast, whose tongue lolls out
and licks your frozen body,
                    your ice-clad soul
– forgive us our sins –
washing in long caresses, massaging in warm waves,
until the heart's rhythm slowly accelerates,
and the silence step by step
                    passes...
Gurgling gutturals come
from the radiant darkness of your insides,
where salt crystals once again chime their glass-like song.
You reach out a flower from the moon's furthest region,
                                        wake
from your deeply lethargic state to a – where to?

The Genie Out of the Bottle

Was Eve a completely identical twin created
                                  from Adam's white ribs
by a particularly imaginative cell scraping
– or did Zavos and an Antinori read
the story of Genesis too literally,
so that perhaps they escaped from difference, time and death?
When sheep and cattle and goats, pigs and mice
can be duplicated easily and without an alibi,
we too can surely be produced on an extremely lavish scale...
What future will take us by surprise,
if rows of clones go wandering around snow-blind
greeting one another, for copies don't
have pairs of parents who themselves
tell passionately how they sinned with pleasure
in a garden's shadow centre, there where their kisses
were heavy drops of rain on the earth
                                  – seen from the sky
or stars high in the sky
                    – seen from the earth.
When the first green breeze of spring will tug
hard at the always waking walls of the heart's muscle,
boy-clones will fall in love with crater-deep
wounds of longing infatuated with their own mothers,
and girl-clones with a flash of lightning lit within their breasts
blindly fall in love with their own fathers, while new couples
– possessed by the thought of a fixed identity
and with a need for endless future traces –
ready-tested stand in line with the desire
to see themselves spectacularly portrayed
so as one day to have a little ego-clone —
as soon as, screened and quality controlled,
highly paid, but as a legal experiment,
                              it can be put into what world?
– where a worn-out Venus slowly fades.

IV

A priori expectation

The Whales in Paris

It's probably not Paris that the whales sing about in the great oceans,
but the city is beautiful this morning, where I wake up
after dreaming about ton-heavy, cavorting whales.
On all sides they swam, the gigantic creatures,
my only salvation in the rough sea
was to grab hold of their tails, which were so slippery
that my hands slid the moment the whales altered course
or flapped their tails hard, hurling me far away,
but each time I swam back, grabbed hold again
and in this way managed to survive all night...
On the wall opposite I see now that it's a brilliant morning,
the greetings of the birds suggest the same,
the whales are gone, a woman moves from window to window,
raising the Venetian blinds and opening the windows ajar,
– this I enter in my dream journal.
The sun falls into the woman's kitchen,
where she walks around putting heaps of clothes together.
Each day our lives are invented;
a so far new combination of the known and unknown,
will perhaps arise today —
it depends on what falls into our minds,
falls into us, embraces us with memory-deep gaze,
when we seek an entrance to something
                              that is freedom for the soul —
and will tolerate no limit other than the open sky.

Rue Vieille du Temple

Even at two in the morning the sparrows sing in March,
they flutter amorously around between the walls
as I stagger home from the bar, where the pulse
thuds beneath the skin, hard and waiting —
and the darkness gleams
                  star-fragrant, tight-fitting,
flows like silver
         and glass plasma,
as the men kiss one another.
In the morning in the café, while standing
but without haste I drink a cup of coffee,
a man and a woman at a table share another cup.
I watch caresses fall from his free hand
towards her ear, neck and hair,
I see the silence rise from ankle to nape.
Here no one will find my hand,
I fall asleep to the sound of a burglar alarm
from a parked car in the street.
Like Ariadne's thread stretched out in the labyrinth
the screaming contracts through my sleep,
                      ruby red...
I live on love for love
        in a priori expectancy.

Journey Without End

Close my eyes, hear the silence waken —
a river boils beneath the sky, goes roaring off,
images wrench themselves free from an inner continent,
fizz past in confusion.
What I see, I can't hold on to:
The thought, the dreamed, the not-yet born,
the far, the near, the much-desired
                              – the whole of it
I let go of,
allow the images to be what they are.
They sail away, slip from my field of vision,
the water washes past my closed eyes.
I roll the images out, empty them all into the river,
until there is nothing left
                        except the heart, which can be heard,
except the lungs, which breathe
                        – in, out...
It's not I who must get moving,
but the river, as I sit by its bank.
A light-shower of pearls the river becomes,
a water-light that trembles – the heart
scarcely needs to beat –
a mirror-undulating light, a freely cascading water,
which no grille shall block.
There's a tingling in my skin, a faint pulsing,
and inside the light, the purple blue
in a living flame,
and inside the purple blue
                        an eye
which sees
that I give in and disappear,
give in and appear,
sees that the river becomes light, the light becomes haze,
that the mist wraps around me,
enfolds me
        in a remembered embrace,
that I am slowly filled with emptiness, that the river
has glided out of my field of vision, that nothing reaches me,
that my body is heavy, heavily floating,

that the light vibrates white,
                    before it stands still —
that there's a humming and stinging under the roots of my hair,
as I come to myself,
                    light as the mist
that rises from the earth in the early morning,
                              – open my eyes
and consider the world: Mysteriously near, and crystal sharp.

Pulsating Planet

Inversely proportional to the soul's black holes
is illuminated Paris
seen on the clearest nights from the top of Montmartre —
where everything that can sparkle
radiates and pulsates in the darkness
from towers and domes to streetlights, advertising signs
                              and bedside table lamps —
gleam by gleam the gaze is shifted
ever further out into the horizon's sphere
– or the city sensed on rainy nights
with more than 7,000 flashes,
                    which in a fever-alphabet
flare up – and vanish without trace
in contrast to time,
which prints its visibly hurled signs
around my eyes...
Swaying in a gust of wind on the edge
of the narrow stone steps of a steep staircase,
I read beneath a waxing moon
the distilled zigzag script of wild graffiti
written with burning ciphers on the sky,
where blinking planes in slow motion
move a full stop,
          – break the code,
but only to be touched
by a generous infinity,
              lost,
like the small boy on the bank of the Seine
who loudly spelled his way through his schoolbook
and for the first time in his own language
was able to break into Aladdin's cave
to mysteriously glowing fruits
                    and other hidden gifts.
Who wants to kill the dreams here?
                    Find the perpetrators!

Sleep Hieroglyph

One moment,
when others are out of sight,
in the dream you will embrace me,
so that my plutonic soul
will not forget that I'm alive.
You throw your arms round me,
in that same instant push
up into me —
my white heart
beats hard
in the rose darkness.
I adapt myself to a foreign climate,
am surprised by your smell, which I didn't know,
but love unconditionally,
like something I had missed without being aware of it,
as the earth goes under,
                   and you are the sky,
where a rising sun
          shines
behind the horizon of your closed eyes...
My heart beats hard as a volcano,
the blood's lava glows through my sleep,
writes itself somatic-black down the sides of the mountain.

V

Critique of incestuous thinking

Critique of Incestuous Thinking

If fish had words, they would have told of us, of a summer
when we shot through the water,
my father and I —
broke wave after wave, as they opened in cascades
                              of rain and fear.
I lay on his back, hung on his shoulders
with my arms thrown tight around his neck.
He swam – which I hadn't learned to do,
I followed each stroke, watched his muscles move
supply tensed under the skin.
With his energy we cleaved the waves, which were far colder
than my blood, with his energy I came to love the water,
and the warm touch of the air.
My father's gleaming back, up and down,
                              forward, forward
His arms in the surface of the water in great, powerful jerks,
while I lay feverishly still, until his movements became mine...
He hurled himself forward, I closed my eyes tight shut,
he dived, and I was there, too —
pressed my arms more tightly round him, as we flew under the water,
secure with the strength of muscles, when we shot away,
bobbed up, rushing on towards nothing
other than the joy of the terrifying, and the horizon that curved.
It was a journey not from A to B,
but from catacomb-like dream
                              to lightning play
through drops' splashes of fire.
The smell of his skin blended mirages and sea-sharp salt,
like that I glided over fathomless forests of seaweed and mountains
        of stone,
away over a white, rippled sandy bottom, just as once
on an open sea he was borne
on his mother's back, with his arms around her neck.
Like that we dived again and again, like that I learned a firm grip,
but also to let go where nothing is certain —
to dance with the words,
                    break sound barriers of water
                                        and sing with whales.

Like that I passed through oceans' ineluctable routes of pain,
learned that, though probably drowning, I still soared —
Like that I met the men: We would dive
down to caves in the cliffs, to hidden grottos, rise
from the deepest sea, dream
of ebb and flow
        listen to the beat of fins,
listen to the pulse... Towards death – keep us flying in sun, salt
    and foam.

Season for Game Hunters

The hunting rifle lies on the hat shelf
behind the row of headwear
for civilised use.
It wasn't lions that crept around
or hid behind the dolmen.
We shot at
tin cans, which hung
dangling down from the apple trees,
practised
so as not to maim the creatures,
while the dogs howled in the village.
But the kick from the rifle-butt
was too brutal
for a girl's shoulder...
I had a hunter's eye,
but decided to aim
                at something else.
I let game be game,
cuddle you diagonally
with sharp objects,
I lose what I have,
but receive something precious in return,
though I don't know
what it is —
but wait and wait for it
and am afraid
– how else would I summon up courage?
The air is full of wings
and cries, a mud of excrements.

Does the Infinite Grasp Our Longing?

Earth is lifted and turned in a heavy slurping, gulls wheel and spin
a movable net around my father
                              from here —
and out in the distance, where the forest is fading all around.
My gaze follows him over the field along the straight furrow,
until he is only a dot
                        that moves...
High above, clouds glide slowly across the sky,
the sun rushes forward, scrapes
against hands and cheeks, against the black earth,
into which the ploughshare thrusts deep,
until with a slam the blade
strikes hidden stones so that the sparks go flying,
and the sun
makes the bare stones shine uniform as siblings,
but also different on closer inspection.
The space expands with every breath,
                                    the sun is obscured again.
I read the back
            one way,
the face at a long distance and turned towards me
                                            the other way,
until the cold penetrates up through the boots.
The tractor approaches, the noise and the screaming gulls.
Sticky, massive odour,
as the mouldboards turn the earth,
                                the day-side to the night-side.
His concentration in raising the plough, turning round
and lowering it without losing speed,
                                without catching my gaze.
– What glacier brought the earth we are bound to,
but from which gulls tear themselves free
and draw their screaming over,
                            threads of sound
painted in Jackson Pollock-like hurled movements,
closely filtered together as they hover around tractor and plough —
a low-hanging cloud of white wings.

My father to and fro... furrow after furrow...
From sun to moon... From roots to wings...
My pencil over the paper,
                    ploughing its way through the whiteness,
while the plough
        writes a poem longer than time.

VI

Symptom cycle with birds

Farewell, We Say

Farewell, we say to the dying,
but don't forget them,
                until we ourselves die,
and are perhaps remembered
so as that way – while grey ducks
in a pointed vibrating wedge
migrate across the sky —
                to receive continued existence.
Just as the words, when they are spoken,
receive meaning and brilliance.
Or the grain of dust that hangs in the beam of light,
makes visible the fact
that the globe with its six billions
goes on rotating —
                and nothing seems impossible.
Exactly as when my father
walked with me holding one hand
while my mother held the other...
So with bare feet I passed
the snake in the grass and the worst enemies.
So I was brought floating into the world,
into the open
                to be deposited here.

In Someone Else's Dream

Between the tree's weavings of stems,
the sun stands in fever-bright dance,
birds sing with requited love.
I intercept waves of sound —
the branches sway in rhythm,
reflexes of morning light are thrown
in across the floor in springy fields of light,
where the cat with a soft thud
settles down to lick a paw.
I'm outside everything, an ear
                            in someone else's dream.
I am hammer and anvil,
raise houses
        parallel-displaced
to the brain's architecture,
knock the words together
                    and hear a brittle sound of wings,
as when I learned how to cut the pages of books,
and be able to make the knife
                        whisper on the paper
like wing-beats through the room...
See birds land on the sills
of kaleidoscopic dwellings,
so tightly that they can hold onto thoughts —
and at the same time so permeable
that stars and other dreams
want to force their way in... Wildly transparent.

Wings, Throat Blood, Snake in Sight

Is it the formula for black holes
we seek to find... Are we losing our grip
and entering
    where nothing is
with oxygen-deficient questions?
The birds here, whose colours reflect
the fauna of innermost dreams,
are busy cruising hieroglyphically
through the air in all directions.
They're carried by currents in the wind,
they whirl in the light, as words roll about the tongue,
circle around one another, slip sideways
and ascend into the wind...
Why explore these holes
or the possibly even larger abysses of the mind,
the darkly undulating and never forgotten,
which flails and struggles under all being —
as long as what has two wings
rises and stays hovering
above a planet in continuous motion.
And I like everyone else
              lose myself,
when these thorny bird-voices sound,
when they call loudly and without cease
from hiding places in the trees around.
Or populate the sky like an open songbook,
in order suddenly to plunge
              and dive hungrily
after a snake in the rustling grass.

Gravitation of Shadows

The children play by the lake in throbbing heat.
They touch one another's hands,
the sun from the highest sky
                        makes wounds clot.
The children tumble about in the grass,
spun into dreams —
they stick together like wounds that are healing
and don't even know
                        they are angels...
They kiss one another, they cuddle,
they go near the water.
The plants on the bottom glow in the sun
for the ones who tread right up to them.
In from the path the plants can hardly be sensed in the water
and not by the ones who are moving further away
in among the trees' forgetfulness.
The children play by the lake —
they gather what they find,
they scream with delight and take it with them.
The green swaying on the bottom
emerges from the low water,
sucks them down towards a darkness
                        they have no name for.
Birds fly above them,
the shadows from the birds
                        give the children wings...
But the season changes
            and becomes another,
the place changes
            and becomes another,
                        the era another.

Skull-white Frosty Day

The birds of passage seek to be away, Europe is one big poem,
where one stanza is sung in one land, another in another.
The earth's crust has stiffened, the earth's heart
hard cement.
Naked stones are covered
                        by a tear-fine film of rime.
In order to live
we must bear
harm we inflict on one another,
                        often unwittingly.
From the sky's grey frosty light
the snow comes whirling
carried by an easterly wind.
A snowflake on your lips,
death's
gleam —
even when you smile, and with your gaze
perforate the sealed landscape...
Dreams pulsate through stabbing cold,
wake slumbering prehistoric animals to life in us.
Prisms of ice and quiet lightnings,
                        you exist in my eye.
Bird-shadows draw long trails:
Denmark, Germany,
                France, Spain, Portugal...
The birds live where the light is...

VII

Passages

In the Lottery

Das Labyrinth ist der richtige Weg für den,
der noch immer früh genug am Ziel ankommt.

WALTER BENJAMIN

In the lottery I won the right to silence,
voluntarily let my mouth fill with sand,
which flowed from many hands
                    like a sealing of the tongue.
Let myself be led into that room assigned as a dwelling,
                                        ascetic,
no bigger than a cubby-hole.
The door was closed by a friendly person,
bowls of food appeared,
                    enough for the whole day
and books by Edgar Allan Poe and Dylan Thomas.
These feverish days were a ladder
                    without steps.
A large bird settled on a branch now and then
outside a window right at the top,
put its head on one side, stared with one eye
                            into my numbness
and flew away...
The same dog repeated its howling evening after evening,
as though it were caught in a fox trap, not far off.
Sepulchral darkness of ravens' wings were the nights,
when they closed round me, fixed me
                        in immobile positions.
Death
is learned patiently, I thought,
and put my head to the door when someone knocked —
but then the sound of visitors' steps had already vanished,
like echoes lost in labyrinths of labyrinths,
today had long ago turned into yesterday...
I had to let the time pass, but woke up and heard voices,
opened the door
which to my furious astonishment
                    had not been locked!
A garden which has not given up its dream
spreads out before my feet now

57

in a kaleidoscope of reflected light —
bushes flower, sending wet flashing scents towards me,
rainbow-coloured birds streak in ciphers through the air,
under the trees people move about talking,
energetically deciphering a new plant.
The door bangs to behind me,
singing I go outside,
        go to meet your familiar faces.

Diving

A fly rolls forward
        big as a whale
light flickers —
I climb and climb with the creature
between cloud crests of waves.
I wake, can't sleep
half the night, a new millennium
has started at the bottom of my soul.
My skin is warm, and you
climb and climb,
        until the creature suddenly dives
and quickly hurls itself up again...
You give me a drink
of tall and salty foam,
of snow-white beginning.
A sea of uncontrollable atoms opens
above conical glasses
on tall stems, words
grow through the night
towards a first dawning in the east,
the earliest morning colours of apotheosis.
I am hip and shoulder,
I am nape and heel,
a kernel of ice
melts in your sun,
        supersonic.
Into me you fall
        and fall —
I am a final sky for your landing.

Knowledge

In the light of the soul's dream the chestnut's leaves are hammered
by the sun to gold,
the tree throws them off, but the pigeons in the elm tree
have erred and have young now,
                                and you
are a tower of happiness and threatening expectation.
You illumine the strongly scented leaf,
raise me in a spiral with your gaze.
The sun behind driving rain clouds,
the sun in a semi-circle around us,
from window to window, dizzy
as the blood murmurs in the finest capillaries:
                                The silence sings,
but we don't suffer from fear of heights,
we climb stiffly,
                crowned by crows' cawing,
balance and climb further in the gale,
which is mild as a springtime, as hands and lips,
but comes towards us in gust after gust,
while all around collapses —
                        falls
to the earth, where the wet darkness grows
in yawning chaotic formations...
We may lose each other from sight again,
but like the intense colours
                        the blind man sees in his sleep,
the skin wants to remember where it was touched,
by a zigzag of flying hands, by roaming lips,
by a tongue that suddenly travels
to places surprisingly authentic and obscure,
as though it wanted to know the end before the beginning.

Warning

Don't fly kites, when you have me
and at the slightest breath
                    the rain-rushing sound
from my waking dreams...
Our meeting-place is five parts of the world,
but there are also inner spaces, my love,
with magnetic fields where compasses lose their way,
there the descent begins step by step
towards the light-depths of continents,
                        there we save our lives,
listen to the blood's storm
and grow primordially old,
                    yet not without nourishment.
You are here, I am here – both acutely listening,
but the needle-like trembling that leaps out,
does not exist without our vulnerability.
So if the world around us is wise,
it may forgive us
for hiding in the open, for being naked,
for opening our eyes and speaking,
that our thoughts together may make sense of what
is transformed
    in constant succession,
when we drown our hot bodies in cooling fire —
remembered by seething maple trees whose leaves
fall in flying glints, hurl yellow and red
into the autumn's diamond night,
where yours is mine
                and vice versa,
in there where the firewalls of the soul
can no longer keep spaces apart.

Burning-point of Oceans

'No Fishing'
    it says there on the sign beside the curved ocean,
but I have just caught
        a whale
without being swallowed —
it's the words that hold the whale in my mouth now.
In the light,
which is grey like human ashes,
I think about the whale's being
– realise,
while the earth is kissed
by metal-hot rain,
that nothing is what I have expected.
There is no other centre in a seasick world
than everything that freely moves...
What did the whale's
eye catch?
From the primordial sea it threatened me
with a crater's joy,
        with holy shamelessness.
To my relief it fills
infinitely more than my own life,
when I dream about it
– or in order to exhaust the limits of the possible
encounter it fever-naked
        and notice
as the miraculous glows and hurts,
that I'm losing my soul in its,
        because it is losing its in mine.

Only What Hasn't Happened Can't Be Lost

It's overcast, and the silence breaks free:
The humming-bird's dream, the whale's dream
– do they have a common denominator,
apart from that both have seen your happiness?
— Don't wake me
    with your disappearance...
The humming-bird stands still in the air
                            with whirring wings,
a quivering forms my brain.
The humming-bird sucks honey
and is named 'The one that kisses the flower'.
Your lips touch my face,
you probably mistake me for a dusty flower,
or I flower in free fall between your hands,
float so deep
that I lose myself in the protective darkness
                            of oceans.
The blood smells strongly of blood,
I have seen a whale and travel with you
in deafening embrace
            of the created.
Between angular continents our glowing trails move,
we survive in the sea's wilderness
between night and day and condensed memory
under foam-grey sky.
— Don't wake me
    with your disappearance...
The humming-bird's dream, the whale's dream
– do they have a common denominator
apart from the fact that in the flash of magic mirrors both
have seen our happiness bring it all to nothing?

These Wild Flowers

The walls are cracking, the city is awake,
here we are grown-up children
being sucked further into
the darkness.
Drizzle, caresses,
wetly gleaming,
night-silent streets.
And down there along the quay
the cold smell of the cobblestones'
velvety granite,
which under the streetlamps
mirrors the sky's
lacquer-black bed.
The light spins soundlessly
a net-fine veil
           around the one who kneels...
Drizzle, caresses,
the fire-plant's flames —
the tongue captures silver snow.

An Optimistic Version of Duchamp

The air above Paris
                lives a life of its own,
there your smell hangs —
and only the smell can be separated from the body
and still have existence.
Your smell is still here – it doesn't deceive,
but spreads its rings
like a chemical vibration in the air
                              I breathe in
on this overcast day of damp roof slates
and slanting raindrop patterns down the windowpanes,
like an indomitable remnant
after an astronomically complex division sum
we happily tried to solve...
Your smell has torn itself free
and set its satiated, colourless trace,
                        has become the centre
of your vanishing, which like a speechless universe
seeks me out in order to connect you with me...
I breathe in, the heart continues its beating,
I'm not to fill my life with poisonous thoughts,
but apparently with attentive gaze
                        look forward
to a later inevitable arrival —
the hemisphere of a final shocking beginning.

It's Your Face That I Seek

It takes an ever stronger light to thread a needle
to sew on a button that popped off my blouse
during a deep sigh —
at the sight of two young men who, chained with
handcuffs to a railing, from which
in the clear weather – with a view
that isn't granted to everyone – they could see
fifty kilometres across the rooftops of Paris,
and as they listened
to the distant sounds of the nuns' choir singing,
were frisked by hefty policemen
and then set free, as boisterous
as the nuns,
who after choral singing and before vespers
played rounders behind Sacré Coeur
in fluttering chalk-white habits and grave-black veils
and then knocked down
stacks of tin cans from an unsteady garden table
jumping with delight when, like a miracle,
the youngest succeeded in scoring a hit just as precisely
as I would like to send the red thread
through the eye of the needle,
but before me see a beloved face,
as in a metamorphosis it changes
from one expression to the opposite:
I have a strong will,
                    it says,
                        but also a strong desire...
Cherchez ma face – sing the nuns
as they think of *Le Seigneur.*
C'est ta face, Seigneur, que je cherche,
they sing – while I,
by the glow of the lamp, with great clarity see yours.

'Sacrifier'

Half asleep we breathe in time turned towards each other,
as though we drew breath with the same lungs —
but two separate bodies
                    are needed in order to shape infinity.
The lips' downbeat in a kiss
against the warm salt of a swaying shoulder.
The May air's sweetness
mingles with acid green early summer in the blood.
We inhale the whiteness, the pureness
— exhale the carbon
Crystal grilles of minerals grow inside us, clear
and weightless. Like a quiet, hard crackling in the mountain.
I count down
           to the darkness and amorphous melancholy,
to the maelstrom of a life
that gives us
our death —
count up
          to light and prismatic precision.
I'm flown through:
First by your moon-fire, then by your morning sun,
— roads of oblivion along which
I'm led further into the real
and received with open arms,
                  led onwards
without understanding why and to what...
In Danish one distinguishes between
to *surrender oneself* and to *sacrifice oneself*,
but it's the same word in French,
                  red and two-edged,
I notice with quickening breath
during an assault in backlight.
A sudden outburst
of your wild-growing adoration
sets its signature of vanishing traces.

We Are Not Creatures of a Single Day

In the darkness the moon keeps watch
concavely.
Your eyes are closed —
everyone has seen something,
but not the same.
What the face conceals,
          the night notices
and the door stands open.
Your eyes are closed —
your face is near to mine.
A power rises and rises
from the moment we are born,
          – and we are not creatures of a single day.
Our brains are not constructed
to guide wings
but to build languages
and navigate in a different way:
to think is to try
to see in a new way, with polar clarity
– which also means
to grasp the limitation.
Your eyes are closed —
your body is a leap forward
into that saffron-glowing radiance.
Sleep has overturned
the Rosetta stone of your brain;
it shows a script
we have not deciphered before...
Our place is time,
and we read,
as though we are trying to remember
what has not yet happened to us.
What we do not do
          is not forgiven.
One hand grips hard,
the other protects,
a third blesses.

Your eyes are closed —
the soul is drawn
by that infinite space,
built from the pauses in the music.
I have your cry
            in my mouth.

VIII

Retrospective penetration

The Book of Generations – Life According to DADA

Abraham begat Isaac and died;
and Isaac begat Jacob and died;
and Jacob begat Judas and his brethren and died;
And Judas begat Phares and Zara of Thamar and died;
and Phares begat Esrom and died;
and Esrom begat Aram and died;
And Aram begat Aminadab and died;
and Aminadab begat Naasson and died;
and Naasson begat Salmon and died;
And Salmon begat Booz of Rachab and died;
and Booz begat Obed of Ruth and died;
and Obed begat Jesse and died;
And Jesse begat David the king and died;
and David the king begat Solomon of her that had been the wife
        of Urias and died;
And Solomon begat Roboam and died;
and Roboam begat Abia and died;
and Abia begat Asa and died;
And Asa begat Josaphat and died;
and Josaphat begat Joram and died;
and Joram begat Ozias and died;
And Ozias begat Joatham and died;
and Joatham begat Achaz and died;
and Achaz begat Ezekias and died;
And Ezekias begat Manasses and died;
and Manasses begat Amon and died;
and Amon begat Josias and died;
And Josias begat Jechonias and his brethren and died,
about the time they were carried away to Babylon;
And after they were brought to Babylon,
Jechonias begat Salathiel and died;
and Salathiel begat Zorobabel and died;
And Zorobabel begat Abiud and died;
and Abiud begat Eliakim and died;
and Eliakim begat Azor and died;
And Azor begat Sadoc and died;
and Sadoc begat Achim and died;
and Achim begat Eliud and died;
And Eliud begat Eleazar and died;

and Eleazar begat Matthan and died;
and Matthan begat Jacob and died;
And Jacob begat Joseph the husband of Mary, and died
of Mary was born Jesus, who is called Christ.
It is life that is playing with you
under a desert-black vault,
voices that call to you,
every birth
        is taking place right now.
It's the world that is coming to see
if your eyes are opening,
if you're awake,
if you're procreating
        and setting your name on the one next to you...
You are one individual
        among billions,
you can hear about everyone who was here —
about everyone who took part in the feast
                        all the way to bright morning.

Domain

Suddenly – as milk boils over
                              in a lonely house
where no one is ready to take the pot off the flame,
suddenly – between what is past
and what is to pass,
when a star lights up the day,
the memory of the crematorium's smoke,
ascending from the chimney —
dimly twisted fossils
                  of naked pillars.
A wave rises,
           light rushes up from the earth.
My sister and I wearing sunglasses,
because we mustn't be seen
as the blind wheels of the hearses roll by,
but would like to say farewell...
The grown-ups give the children salt
when they are thirsty,
only the earth is wet with dew,
and the shadow
beneath flowing white flowers cools the day.

Horizontal Lightnings

The horizontal lightnings are foxes, which with tails erect
cross the road
in the lanterns' swaying light.
The van is full of intoxicated people
who through smells of wet pine forests
are being ferried from Birštonas
back to Gedimo in Vilnius,
hundreds of kilometres along a bumpy road
                                        felt even longer homewards.
Waves of steam hang in the air after the rain,
the raw mist
mingles with the smoke from the cigarettes in the van.
The wine was good,
            so was the amber-golden brandy
                        and then the beers.
The ravens, which up among the creaking of the treetops
shouted out Lithuania's history
above the gravestones at the edge of the wood,
can still be heard.
The midnight discussion in the back seat recalls the flock of birds,
they circled in high spirals between birches, elms and pines,
called me into a trance...
In the grass between the gravestones so overgrown with moss
that they almost came alive,
I gathered long, black, shiny feathers,
moved in among the trees,
where the stone wall had kept the warmth,
after the sun drowned in the forest.
I climbed over the wall,
                  found the way down to the lake.
The frogs croaked on the shore
as in the ponds on the fields of my childhood,
long ago filled in with stones and earth.
Goodbye, songbirds and wild cherries. Goodbye, sticklebacks
removed from a lake in Hellebæk woods
where can fleeing fishes
               swim to?

Goodbye, frogs and flocks of butterflies
Goodbye, dreams. Goodbye, crawling insects
that settled on bare legs
when one walked down to the bushes by the water to taste
the berries which were not blueberries
but bitter
making the tongue contract.
Now barley or wheat is grown there, rape or rye,
harvested on a base of broken masonry and stones
dumped in ponds which day by day found it harder to breathe —
the open closed... Stones sank
and hid a future, while smells and sounds
                              vanished.
A spinning light was doused... Silence took over,
as though someone had written the story of their life
                                   in flint-sharp shadows.

Between Us

The snow on the branches, the snow is shining,
a snow-white path between the trees,
listen, listen,
      a bell of silence...
The cold tugs bitterly at one's nose,
a snow-white smell plucked from the sky
which rapidly turns grey, a creaking path
beneath the growing darkness of the spruces,
don't be afraid,
      stop bawling!
A snow-white darkness inside the forest,
where we can no longer recognise the path,
after the sun's rosehip-coloured plunge
deep into
      where no one can hear us shout.
A growing forest, where the blind lead the blind
– and then suddenly a path
which after all leads back to lit windows,
to the garden
where the snow has settled
like manna in the desert, like small white frogs,
like porous happiness, like the dreams in the cold
and taste of honey for forty years...
A snow-white smell plucked from the sky,
the door opens:
      To be expected —
the warmth inside and the cold air which in a gust
blows in from outside,
the voices all round and lighted candles.
I crept in to the grown-ups,
to their warm and sweetish smells.
Give time —
the snow is shining
the snow casts white shadows inside one's veins,
a long sigh into the darkness where I lie, listening.
Dully humming insects, seconds,
           humming seconds,
the cold outside, the warmth indoors,

the night freezes, the earth freezes
                    loudly —
granite-heavy wedges of pain race through the body
in a delta of asymmetrical paths
                    which lead everywhere
– and back to the heart's hammering silence.
The black, frosty earth still doesn't cover its mouth,
the words are streaming from it,
                    do you hear them?

Fossil Sleep

Your darkness, your light, your crystals of life,
the silence on your temples
                    as on a blossoming branch.
Vague swells beat in against the shore,
pebbles are sucked
in a lengthy rattling back into the sea.
You are beyond yourself,
while perhaps your recapitulate days and nights
and in a gleam
gather them into a single figure,
                    one only graspable by you.
We dig in the sand... More darkness.
We bathe and sense
waves of cold throb against our lungs.
The sound of the gravel at the edge of the water
mingles with our voices in the tepid breeze,
the breast filled with sea air,
                    a space of purity.
Your darkness, your light, your delta of memories
on the way inwards in a flood of forgetting.
We are with you, we read your journey,
                    before you leave us.
Warm sand trickles from a clenched fist,
drifting clouds...
The death-
light
startles up like a transparent radiance, before death
arrives.
The sky darkens in your rib-cage,
grains of light are extinguished there... Angular clarity of crystals.
Swells beat silently in, uninterrupted,
salt-saturated sea-smells make us drowsy.
I hold your hand,
am one with your warmth.
Among the gazes we, who sit with you,
exchange for one brief second,
                    you disappear —
one world parts from another.

The door is locked, the windows hasped shut,
but there must be a crack in the summer?
How did you get away, we were with you, after all...
Your mouth is open... That way!
We're here... We're breathing,
we embrace one another with relief
as after a well-endured birth,
but we didn't give birth,
                    we gave a living person the slip,
and he was sucked back, into
a universe of openness.
We finish building the sandcastle in the sun,
dig canals and make bridges,
the breeze slowly becomes colder.
We get up, have regained our age
and see the dead body,
                    a stone
shrouded in its own shadow.
You aren't here any more,
                    a genetic murmur in the blood.
Your darkness, your light, your fossil sleep —
the storm-leap into the whiteness.
Never more your voice,
calling us in from the edge of the water.
Death
has struck roots —
you are where the dreams are:
                    Into our future
                              you have gone.
A silver-grey seagull sways and drifts towards land
borne by a wave.
We get up and go, the wind sweeps over the beach,
effaces our footprints in the sand.
The twilight in the room
has inaudibly grown to a portal of darkness,
                              it's only we
                                   who shine.

IX

Dream time

Happy Hour

Given: A stream – and chimpanzees sit down
to follow the flowing,
        listen to the white purling
rising quietly —
      as if heard from music.
So thoughtfully the animals sit
spread in clusters at a distance from one another around the water,
which keeps the dream afloat
          by falling
            over black rocks.
The chimpanzees peer ahead of them,
sunk in themselves
with their backs to the world,
to the intrusive mass of human beings
who with shouts and waving arms
try to provoke more animal sides
in the animals, which with the sun in their coats
are far inside a brooding,
        and won't let anything affect them...
We are apparently not alone in
subtly considering the earth's creation,
listening to whispering stones and flashes of light in the water
– or what makes the chimpanzees
vie with the most persevering philosophers,
when in hours of sensitive thought activity
they sit almost motionless,
        clearly seeing
in fragrant sun-grass by the water,
which flows away with such bubbling, enticing sounds
that for a time they make up for any hostility in the group
– among the public, too,
        among us, who are slowly filled
with breathless wonder at being allowed to witness this unfathomable
    more.

The Dream's Privilege

The air shimmers with the heat of a temple fire,
there where a red-brown, buffalo-like ox
stands on a shore near the water's edge.
Azure-green mountain slopes fade
into the distance on one side, the sea
quietly washes in on the other, mirror-blue.
It isn't my fatherland,
but I am a bird in the air along the coast.
I seek in a straight line frontally towards the ox,
                                        a white bird,
which approaches and is swallowed
by the heavy creature.
It grows wings... The ox in the sand
                        grows enormous wings.
I don't fight with beak and claws,
am on the contrary overjoyed at the sight of the creature,
even though I've been swallowed...
I don't drown in a restless darkness
to the sound of swaying pulse-beats,
                        but wake
in the clearest imaginable light
and observe the ox from outside —
it stands so quietly in the sun with white wings.
It is not an intolerable pain to be swallowed,
just a journey that does not end,
an echo that resounds in the limitless,
one of those transformations
                that make it possible to see
what survives the embraces of a tumultuous life.

The Silence After Us

31/12/1999

There is one day left – and a wild, primeval space in the brain expands:
I put my ear to the warm wall, remember the beating of my mother's heart,
but hear the hum of voices, murmuring of languages now disappeared.
With sunlight Ayers Rock – Uluru – burns from inside,
with wisdom absorbed through six hundred million years...
Dreamed up from the earth the giant rock lies in desert-flat terrain,
like an iceberg its massive single fragment shoots up from the water,
booming several miles of weathered peak to the horizon.
Out of the darkness the stone's back is sung forth by birds in the dried-up scrub,
from trees or nesting holes deep in the wall, until colours change their mind,
and the rock is lifted high by wing-beats, swathed in cries and song,
in pungent morning odours, in a silence clear and endless as the plain,
where I dwindle to a grain of dust and whirl away into the cloud.
Wind and waterfall erode the sandstone rock, whetting, filing,
honing labyrinths of structures, digging oval holes in the foot of the arkose
painted with a sacred script, forming fissures, deep veins and signs:
A cranium-shaped relief, one mouth that weeps, another with a crooked grin...
The reddish brown rock listens, emits echo-notes, sound
of days behind yesterday; rooms that were made by walking along spiral-
and circle trails in dreamt-of times, when things were given names and existence,
and all the new was still as yet obscure, drops of an unseen swarm.
A hallucinated stream of voices reaches me through the wall,
first as chaos, then as the magnet draws iron filings to itself,
gathering them in floating patterns of poles, like the cortex of the brain,
that wants to remember the river between mineral and man – but breaks.
Birds are quiet, the darkness opens and descends on the desert plain;
again it's ocean-black night, and day, the rock is seen by us
who arrive, decipher, dance, dwell, die —
it's we who make the time – I think in cold, raw saurian air,
while a fleeting shower of fire-rain falls, thoroughbred stars in a mass cascade...

NOTES

Kernel: A dialogue with the Sisyphus myth of Albert Camus.

Three Replies to Derrida: These replies concern the lectures given by Jacques Derrida in Paris in 2000 at the École des hautes études en sciences sociales, and also his book *Donner la mort* (1999).

The Genie Out of the Bottle: Written on the topic of cloned human beings. The Italian gynaecologist and embryologist Professor Severino Antinori and his American colleague Professor Panayiotis Zavos met in Rome on 9 March 2001 to discuss their cloning plans with colleagues. At the meeting, Zavos is reported to have said: 'The genie is out of the bottle and will be controlled.' (*Information*, 9 March 2001). Published in *Politiken*, 18 August 2001.

The Whales in Paris: The whale motif is anticipated in the poem 'Moving Sculpture' in my collection *Sekundernes bro* (The Bridge of Seconds). The poem was inspired by David Bowie's 'Heroes', and represents a continuation of my 'conversation' with the poet Michael Strunge.

Passages: The idea of 'passage' from one state to another has pre-occupied me from the first collection of poems I published, and it's no accident that bridges and gates have been appearing in the titles of my books ever since. 'The poem is a possible meeting place,' I wrote in my Poetics. I have focused on passages that make meeting possible or give access to concentration and absorption. Contrary to this is Walter Benjamin's project in *Das Passagen-Werk* (The Arcades Project), in which he attempts to capture the fleeting and the distracted, things that have many forms and are fragmented. I feel an affinity with both forms of perception. For me, the dizzying accumulation of rapid impressions often gives me a perspective on deeper matters. At any rate, *Das Passagen-Werk* was top of my reading list during the writing of *The Whales in Paris*, which contains obvious and hidden connections with Benjamin's work.

Burning-point of Oceans: Incorporates a line from Pindar's Third Pythian Ode, which Camus uses as the epigraph to his essay *The Myth of Sisyphus*: 'O, my soul, do not aspire to immortal life, but exhaust the limits of the possible.'

'Sacrifier': Another greeting to Jacques Derrida, inspired by a lecture he gave at the École des hautes études en sciences sociales in March 2001.

The Book of Generations – Life according to Dada: Based on the St Matthew Gospel, 1.1-1.17.

TARKOVSKY'S HORSES

INTRO

Darkroom on Immanuelkirchstrasse

A storm is coming,
a silence
  whose echo
is played back in the brain.
Whispering it starts here
in the inner ruined city
among the cinders,
where nothing
is —
except the blood-depth's pulse,
one night in Berlin,
and a piece of
star-white paper, filled
with *something* that wants to be called
                              forth.
I linger
in the darkness. Hesitate...
The moon illuminates the skin,
or crash-lands its rays
                    coldly,
just as I'm locking other things out
to be reached by what
for one tense moment
              opens its delta:
Will Eurydice fetch
              her dead father —
like Orpheus sing
of what's lost?
Eurydice, memory,
the eruption.
Before the serpent in the sun
                        struck,
Eurydice did have a life, after all.

GROTESQUES OF FORGETTING

The Wheel

The west-facing panes of the stable
gather the sun's rays
one mild evening
      of swallows.
Round and round they chase
           in a ring
around the tree amid the courtyard.
Round and round,
      my father
holds my head tight
with both hands, no answer,
         makes me
stare in
at the stone wing's sharply illuminated windows.
A needle pricks a hole,
the swallows cry white.
– Look!
says my father.
– Look, the sun!
It isn't the courtyard
going up in flames but me
who's dazzled by the light in the glass.
All of a sudden I'm certain:
My father doesn't know
         what he's doing.
Against the wheel —
my head rests,
      the horses
have torn themselves free.
Long-legged flight
        towards a black horizon.

Trees Are Read

There are always trees that can tell my father
what season we're in, they glow
in his brain,
      the white trunks of the birch trees,
heroically straight
or calmly swaying.
There are trees without leaves,
– so it's winter, when the sun's rays
cut through the room.
There are trees with deep green foliage
– so it's summer, when it's getting dark,
and if the leaves are turning yellow
                it can only be autumn.
Whether it's today
or fifty years ago,
      what is the difference?
Whether two hours have passed
or two minutes,
      is it really important,
as long as shelter is sought
in a glass-clear memory from childhood?
Whether it's me or my mother
sitting in the chair,
      what does it matter?
Whether it's my sister or me,
does it change anything,
      as long as we're comfortable?
The climbing shadows
are so far away that they can't be perceived.
The shadows don't mean a thing,
for at this moment a squirrel is darting
from branch to branch in the cherry tree,
      and *that* we can see.
The birch trees' branches flail newly-sprung,
it is *now* that matters.
Now
there is stillness here, *now*
the sun is shining in through the window,

it's getting warm in here, it is *now*
                                  we're alive...
But what happens
when the trees are pulled up
                              by the roots —
when they drift slowly out
                             where stars are asphalted over?

A Dog Is Let In

My father throws the door wide open, the gale
invades his life, the gale
whirls up in his thoughts,
reveals white patches
on the map of memory.
He stands on the threshold, on the edge
of the darkness,
calls the dog, who doesn't
obey his master.
The dog died
            many years ago.
Outside the front door
the world is catastrophic
and extremely complicated.
The war is over, but warriors
are still
spread
across the entire globe.
House searches, denunciations,
air thick with rumours.
It's cold and night-time,
            and the dog
has been outside for far too long...
Will my father no longer turn back
into the person
            I know?
Orders, arrests,
state of emergency.
Time melts,
        is tomorrow already yesterday?
Through an underground passage
I let the dog in
            here —
why
is it necessary
    to understand?
I pat the dog, give it water to drink.

Expulsion from Paradise

The basket is full of grapes,
ripe grapes.
    the wine
my father has drunk
was deadeningly good,
but the woman
he loved
has turned into his mother,
and he into the son of his beloved —
it's time
to live apart together.
The basket is full of grapes,
fermented grapes,
       the wine
my father has drunk
was tart and bitingly bitter,
he knows that he is more
than the body allows,
it hauls him away to
illness and naked decline —
love and anger flow
without warning over each other
The basket is full of grapes,
rotten grapes,
    the wine
my father has drunk
was rank and sour,
whether the sun shines
in the rain
or the rain falls in the sun,
comes to the same thing —
the water on the fields goes on rising,
an acrid stench spreads, raw and smouldering.

Spot Five Mistakes

Simple objects like the wallet
are spirited away,
and the hat and the gloves have vanished
traceless as rain on water.
The light falters.
And where are the address and telephone number
of my mother's parents?
                (they are dead, after all).
The mirror is so still, so indecisive,
when my father glances into it.
The whole room spins backwards
around a word
in a silent sentence.
Logic has fled
           over the mountains of norms,
even simple obvious words
                have flown away
on distended wings.
Everything whirls in towards the centre,
stretches —
           in waves towards the infinite.
But the grammar still dwells here,
and the pulse beats.
The emotions survive miraculously,
                the hands gesticulate.

Prison Rose

My mother is driving in the wrong direction, my father snorts,
she replies blindly: This is
                              the right way.
He has a tractor parked quite near here,
he says hoarsely,
just as the car is passing a field.
What's lost is lost, the September
sky hangs heavy, my father
doesn't want to get out when we reach the nursing home.
Why should we enter the house of people we don't know?
Why are we being welcomed here?
My father says polite hellos,
brightens up
when my brother comes to meet us —
my brother has bought a fine place.
Or is it my mother's? Has she moved, then?
Has he been sent into exile? Is it a hotel?
My father *didn't* ask for a vacation,
but here he's to live. Bed, table, chair.
Come... My mother places a vase on the table,
red roses from the garden, from a lost
country...*die Niemandsrose*. Come.
Thorns, scratches, blood-smelling heads.
A home? An abyss? A conspiracy?
My father's deaf gaze
at the sight of his name on the door.
Has he been taken to a hospital?
                              Or put in prison?
The world is
where my father's eyes are. I show him
                                        exits,
the windows of every room, the doors.
The building is not a prison, I fly
for both of us
              against winds of ice.
A net of silence sinks,
she gathers the broken pieces, gathers his world, my mother.
The roses' floating light.

That she isn't going to spend the nights here
is a riddle,
neither in my father's bed nor on the sofa
                                    will she sleep —
so *is* it a hotel? A hospital? Or a prison?

Forgetting Masters Its Master

The familiar has hidden itself
or changed names
in the dark,
and the morning knows blessedly little about
what yesterday brought.
Everything is perfectly normal,
                              just different.
The words shadow-box,
tumble over, ignored.
My father doesn't want to get divorced
from my mother —
for then how can they
be together?
The fields have been harvested,
the last load of grain
brought in
years ago.
September's first frost-red leaves
light candles
        and fall sharply through the air,
only the dreams rise.
Everything is perfectly normal,
                              just heavy as lead
                                   and the colour of fear.
My father doesn't want to get divorced
from my mother —
for as long as they are both alive,
the world will go on, won't it?
– But we
are suddenly much smaller
than ourselves. And lost for answers.

Domain Loss of the Mind

The residents play memory games
                          for good reason,
hum and sing songs
they don't know they learned
when they were children.
Yesterday has blown away —
together with the yellow leaves
a mild October wind
has swept yesterday under the trees.
– Every day my father packs
his belongings, his gaze
is empty,
   a drained lake.
His breathing is in flight,
he wants out and away,
                          wants to go HOME.
No longer remembers *which one*,
the moments of clarity
are too brief.
– Every day we erase signs of leaving,
put things back in their places:
piles of clothes (washed and ironed),
toothbrush, screwdriver, inch rule,
shaving things, photographs, letters
and extension lead,
                  as though life
could revert to the beginning.
HOME is
         where my mother is.
My father is too old
to be himself.
The naked nakedness
can't be concealed —
we cover him
         with reneging hands.

Pretty Rosi

My father doesn't remember how well-read
                             he is.
In his bookcase I spot
Rilke's *Briefe an einen jungen Dichter*.
Like the first peal of a heavily
floating bell
         one bronze-still morning,
Germany presents itself...
I wanted to visit the girl who was my pen-friend
in spite of protests.
My mother couldn't bear
                the sound
of the German language —
she heard Hitler
         in every word.
During the war like my mother my father was
forced
to flee to Sweden,
but on his shelves in the bookcase
there were German books.
DA stieg ein Baum. O reine Übersteigung!
O Orpheus singt! O hoher Baum im Ohr!
– Remember,
it doesn't matter what family you visit,
said my mother
         and sleepless sent
her sixteen-year-old daughter away,
they all – in different ways
took part in the war.
I understood her pain,
              but wanted to overcome it.
In 'my' family, with Rosi,
              pretty Rosi,
needles could not be used.
Rosi's father
couldn't bear the sight
           of needles —
he saw Hitler
       in every needle.

Rosi's father had been through something during the war
that could not be talked about, not even
in his own house
– that was the first thing the women told me.
If I wanted to sew
            I would have to go somewhere else
like Rosi, her mother and old Oma.
– My father knows something about needles
women don't know,
Rosi whispered one evening
on the way home from the discothèque,
                        where she
and her at least as pretty Gerhard,
on the dance floor
under the brilliance
            of the reflecting glass globe
were chosen as couple of the evening,
without so much as the pop of a button...
DA stieg ein Baum,
Rosi
wanted to dance round and round,
just be allowed
        to live,
but Rosi's father had been through something
to do with needles that burned
                and stuck into Rosi,
something that long after the war was over
                    still kept her father blindingly awake.

The Earth's Rotation

An earthquake in Asia has changed
the earth's rotation —
my father's days
are not just one split second
                    shorter.
He's nearing a ticking eighty,
but doesn't want to be
either an engineer or an architect.
At night my father takes exams,
he wanders around in the corridors
without the slightest idea
                    of whether he has passed.
The days are quiet
as cuts from a whip.
– I sowed the grass here,
says my father, who has recreated
the Garden of Paradise
wherever he was beached.
I look out over the nursing home's sloping lawn.
– Then I planted a hedge,
which can grow so it covers the wrought-iron fencing.
He makes a generous gesture with his arm.
It is my father that I see —
he is a part of the earth,
the earth is a part of him.
The earth's density has increased,
                    the earth is rotating
three microseconds faster now.
I will have no rest
as long as my father gets lost at night
and in the daytime dreams
                    overdosed awake.
The sky
is a white wall,
I lean upwards,
while atomic clocks are adjusted
by more than a leap second.

Flames Freeze

– Here is a picture of you,
my father says, handing me
an unfamiliar photo
of my mother, naked, and quite young.
The air on the edge of the world is thin,
or am I dangerously dizzy?
– And here is our mother,
my father adds cheerfully
handing me a picture
of my grandmother.
Time and space are bright shadows,
                         flames freeze.
I visited
my grandmother again and again
until one day she
took my hand and asked:
– I'm sorry,
but do we know each other?
It takes light eleven minutes and eight seconds
to travel from the Sun to the Earth —
I looked at my grandmother:
            Snow was melting,
a thin film of 37° and the colour of the sky
                         in spite of the war.
I still remember
        everyone I love – – –
The road's dotted line goes on and on
out across the asphalt – further than west,
where the water flows
                long-sighted
and in shiny, radiant tones:
One day
there will *not* be a face to look into —
my father
will lose his soul   to other souls.

Addressee Unknown

For some inexplicable reason
the signs in the district
have been switched about
during the last few months.
The roads have acquired different names,
and the keys don't fit the doors of
                          any of the houses.
The residents have no doubt
been informed by the council.
They *have* been warned, but even so
it isn't easy to get used
to so many new names.
It's too late to turn round,
and who
can find their way back,
when the signs are all different now?
One constantly has one's address changed —
too often, my father says,
and asks the way
                    to his land.
The autumn dryly lifts
the last leaves from the trees,
his eyes
seek protection in mine.
Impenetrable walls are stormed
by an invisible army,
ruined fortresses crumble,
manor houses decay,
dream palaces collapse.
Stables, barns, silos, sheds
and castles in the air come crashing down.
It's hard to know
                where
to send one's letters,
and where one lives... Even in broad daylight.

A River Flows By

Days grow into weeks, but *before*
has vanished for my father,
and *after* doesn't exist.
– I have a writing desk, a green sofa, two chairs
and a white bookcase,
my father explains on the phone.
Weeks grow into months,
a river flows by.
I visit him often in the one room
that now is his, sit
alternately on the green sofa
or one of the two chairs, help
to find
a book on the bookcase or a pen
that is hiding
in the writing desk's inexhaustible drawers.
Full moon after full moon
the water rises arctic.
An astronomical chart can't decipher that swarm
of thoughts which is splintering
                visibly
and stands exposed like the interior of houses
after bombs have fallen in a war.
I know my father,
as the night knows the stars.
With all my might
I try to find
       a bridge between his thoughts.
The river is a bottomless flow
impossible to swim in.
Together
we cross the fleeting bridge —
                walk dry-shod to land.

The Surrounding Space Is a Pause

The flag hangs motionless – and again at half mast,
who it is hoisted for,
                    no one reveals.
It's snowing thickly and silently —
the snow is gathering around the garden, the car park
and the birds' vowels.
These wiped-out borders change
                    the brain's geography.
We sit side by side, listen to the snow
that is piling high outside.
My father's childhood home elides
with later dwellings, they form
one living HOME.
It's moving day for thoughts in the creaking snow,
as they jerk otherwise unbudgeable furniture around.
A parlour in one house connects
with a garret in a second,
a basement in a third.
Every point welds the soul together
into a single *now*,
                    it is today for always.
It's snowing thickly and silently —
the law of gravity was discovered
in a peaceful orchard,
the swinging of the pendulum
within the refuge of a church.
It's snowing thickly and silently —
frost crystals dance
with the lonely speed of comets.
Snow embers, gathered to infinity,
                    count us, too.
The world has lost its colours to the dizziness,
the landscape is vanishing.
There is only us amidst ice-whirling flakes,
so exiled and close to each other,
that only the remoteness of remoteness
remains,
that maelstrom of a grave we in a draught of light
                    stare up into.

A Bench in the Sun

A day in March wrapped up in big coats,
a day of sun
and long shadows
        engraved
in the asphalt of the car park.
My father and mother have walked around
like young sweethearts. Arm in arm.
– We've walked round the world,
my father coughs, hollowly.
– It took a quarter of an hour,
my mother states.
We sit down on a bench in the sun,
my father enjoys the late summer,
                  or is it the winter light?
At that moment the planks vanish
somewhere under me —
I fall and fall.
      Is his brain to be stripped
of one more vision?
I reply with a nod towards the daffodils,
               the yellow light.
One day my father told stories,
from the first paintings on the rock wall of the cave
to rockets sent out into space
– and further, to thoughts
        about not killing hope.
He remembers how
as a child he viewed old age:
He felt sorry for people who got old!
– They're like tall trees
which may topple over
        to all sides,
and they've forgotten the names
of their dogs —
      is it Rolf or Robin or Bonnie?
We sit together on a bench in the sun's zone,
the young pair of sweethearts
and I,
the odour of March spreads, a scentless odour.

The Centre of Attention

My father sees my mother to the door, waves goodbye.
Snip snap snout,
        this tale is out —
for in the wheelchair at the world's end
                        Eva reigns.
She implores my father
for one thing and another, he listens.
She complains of pain, he comforts,
– for *she* is primordially old, and *her* fate
                        is going to be effaced...
My father introduces me to Eva
and all the other residents, as though it's
my fist visit to the nursing home.
In his room I have got the things ready for tea
and to read aloud
from Hans Andersen's
        'The Snow Queen',
but suddenly all plans for stories are changed.
Tip tap tin,
        a new one can begin —
when my father wheels Eva in.
– The strangers may easily become friends
when one has met them, my father says.
The stranger friend in the wheelchair
eats his cakes,
        but they are too hard for false teeth.
Immediately my father looks for different cakes
in the writing desk drawers.
Then Eva throws her love headlong
at the grapes
I've brought for my father,
she drinks from his cup, and he calls her
                        Alma.
Behind *drifting snow* and *cutting winds*
the snow queen waits patiently.

White Bridling

Red blood, white blood, black blood
fills the brain,
          bursts the skull.
The earth cracks, starry night
over my father's harrowed fields,
where seven white horses call us outside
with loud whinnying.
– This drop in memory
is an ocean full to overflowing.
Red blood, white blood, black blood,
there in the field the bridling horses stop —
broken loose
from a travelling circus
                or sent from where?
We have no horses on the farm,
but they have come to *us*!
With no saddles and no riders...
I'm awake,
far into the marrow of my spine,
I'm galloping awake.
The skin's pores open
                and bolt,
the night enters, chill, clear.
I'm blinded
by the moon-white bellies of the horses,
hear their snorting at the sight
of me and my father.
For a descending second
the horses lift my heart
                higher —
than it has ever flown through space before.
Horses ready to leap into the night,
                to leap out.
There is no
No Horses sign,
this planet is a wide-open terrain. Anything can happen.

– An ocean of fire and salt
overflows.
Heavy hoof-beats streak away,
then
insurmountable twilight. Rumbling.

Bottomless Season

Not bird, not fish, the thimble
                    isn't found —
near and far are gone, up and down not there,
like the green tie,
                    that is usually red.
Not the sight of a young man wearing
a freshly ironed shirt
inside the expectant mirror.
Not sounds of horses' hooves in the courtyard, not
a scent-drowning lime tree,
heavily humming with bees,
not grain, seed, rape
and white fields of poppies, comatose,
not a bull
that has torn itself free, not heifers
that must be gathered in
on a meadow beside Esrum Lake, not cows
that must be milked, not a calf
that must be scratched behind the ear, not
cud-chewing calm in the stable
at the sound of a butterfly
                    at a stable window.
Not the animals' rhythm, steered by the day,
not milk from the milk can for half-wild cats
and chaff in the air,
not still-born sucking pigs thrown out
on the dunghill, not the creatures
                    that don't know
                              they must die.
Not mildew, not mould, not spreading
weeds, not chemical poison spray,
not perishing cold rain-sodden summers,
not trees blown down
in the howling of autumn storms.
Not machines that must be oiled,
not tools that must be kept clean,
not a straw stove that must be attended to.
Not sweat and dust and fumes
                    from blue gasoline,

not tractor wheels, which in pouring rain
work themselves down into a mess
of mud and mire,
not beating of arms in biting frost,
not crackling of firewood in the hearth.
Not sowing time,
            not harvest time,
                        not hunting season
with pigeons, hares, pheasants and roe deer,
not a balance sheet to draw up
on squared paper, stumbling
columns of figures, which one year
give a plus, another minus.
Not a spit
deeper, not a furrow
longer.
Not the happiness of again and again... Not the hard work.
Not the sheltered edge of a wood near the coast.
Not a moonlit dune on the shore.
Not waves hypnotically breaking
with the salt smell of sweet seconds,
                        not delusions —
not a harvest festival in late August,
not a new baby
            in May.
Not a woman's scent-burning skin
or an ornament
        to hang round her neck
one North Sjælland night.
Not a single loaf left, not
a single bottle of wine... Light years
vanish in a grain of dust.
Not bird, not fish, one isn't
                finding the thimble —
near and far are gone, up and down not there.
Shadow verbs are lived through,
                    and the signature is not valid.
The mirror of a bottomless season
greets my father:
            Hello.

Of a Life's Dignity

Only a single key remains
of a life's dignity,
the key
to the last room must be tied
to the trouser pocket on a chain.
The wristwatch
my father forgets to wind,
the hands point
            to ever and always.
Calendar leaves
imperceptibly send out
                shortcuts to the dark,
if they're not turned by the nurses.
The radio,
which should preferably play Bach,
is fixed to the classical music station
by sticky tape,
so that the notes won't run
                seven programmes away.
Sealed up in the present I take
my dose of dreams —
listen to the tangle
of long monologues that are never
trivial,
nakedly knowing
        that the blood turns black.
That on this dizzy
            earth
a deadline is given.

Under the Skull

The planet is a chalk-white cranium
filled with war —
and under the skull burns
a life's library.
Clouds kiss the earth
through the open roof...
Heaps of ash grow,
                    powder
of forgetting sprinkles down.
The house has collapsed,
the doorbell doesn't work,
the coat is gone from the hook.
Ach, du lieber Augustin...
The bed stands empty,
                    and my father is not at home,
doesn't respond to shouts.
THE TONGUE IN FLAMES.
Once he had a bride,
but doesn't remember which night,
only that it was after the war
in September,
and as long as 'for ever' lasts.
The planet is a cranium
filled with war,
                    so one had better flee.
Puts on his clothes to travel
and leaves the house.
Unlocks and locks again and throws away the key,
the unknown
        is only streets away,
and *here*
it is too dangerous to be.
Walks and walks
to meet the endless beginning.
THE TONGUE IN FLAMES.
Alles ist weg, weg, weg...
Try to keep my balance, I follow
the trace of wandering tears
                    out into the night.

The trace is alive
and warm.
The planet is a cranium
filled with war.
Good morning in another town —
                              come back!

The Table of Loss

Behind black-and-white photos in ancient albums
my father recalls the sounds
of spring rain, the smells
of fresh-mown hay, the biting of
the first ripe ears of grain in cornfields.
An instant later every detail
whirls up
      in distant nebulae.
My father vanishes, as days
take flight.
There are no figures that cover
loss, no figures
for the taste of summer on the tongue,
newly picked, bursting red cherries.
And in a blizzard
hot steaming cocoa before the fireplace,
when the avenue up to the farm was blocked.
The water, the air, the earth, the fire, my father's
attentive gaze
made me fling myself out
          across an inner gate,
climb high in trees,
      fly
in dreams – – –
I have set some sums
that *won't* add up —
there are steps
     across logic,
solar systems of inexplicabilities.
Even though he's alive,
I'm looking for
      my father in my father...
A rough tongue
licks my hand,
I won't drown
     in a salt tear,
the cat arches its back, it is time for it to be fed.

The Water Acquires a New Form

No, the stories are not remembered,
but are like a gleam
in the eye,
a warmth in the blood.
– One forgets to forget
                    what one has forgotten,
my father growls with a rust-coloured laugh.
A mortal pain
spreads like clouds —
out from the body's centre.
A grey-streaked rumbling of cars can be heard
and the stutter of a moped.
Magpies are building a nest
outside the window,
                    they paddle
in the air with straw and bits of twigs.
I read stories
my father once gave me,
today 'The Little Mermaid'.
My father is on the bottom of the sea,
he reveals, when the door quietly opens
and a nurse brings medicine.
He is where the water is
as blue as the petals
of the prettiest cornflower
and as clear as the purest glass.
– When you read, my father observes,
it's as though the water acquires a different form,
in which I can swim.
He captures the light in the words,
                    adds the last rays
to the porous cerebral cortex
where the night's silence fills language.

Invitation to the Dance

My father talks such obscure nonsense
that I switch on the radio.
– Has sorrow turned into dancing?
A waltz sounds gently in my ears,
but in his
        the music is the foaming of a waterfall,
a mighty roaring pours into his room.
– Has dancing turned into mourning?
With my feet on his feet
                I learned to dance,
one more time and one more time...
I don't know
whether it was to please me,
I don't know,
or to save on lessons
at the village hall,
where the training was done with boys
from the surrounding farms,
                lads
who sweated and creased one's dress.
Later, for those of the permitted age,
another dance continued,
                high-explosive,
smuggled into discothèques,
then navigating in darkness to parties
at the houses of parents one didn't know,
which by morning
        lay in passed-out ruins.
On to concerts of flying serpents
with the Stones, the Doors and Lou Reed
or barefoot in the streets
                racing the Whitsun sun.
I stood in white stockings
                on my father's black shoes,
one more time and one more time...
There was no music,
but he hummed a waltz rhythm, the notes
filled my head,
set my body's yearning fibres
                in motion.

With my feet on the soft leather uppers
I followed my father's steps,
                    we danced round and round
in the room, where years later I
                    capsized —
in a bridal waltz, a veritable dance on volcanoes.

Magic Splinter

That figure, which one windless day
lolls sleeping
with its head against its shoulder
slumped askew
on a white plastic chair
out on the patio, is it really
                    my father?
He so badly wants to tell me
what he has forgotten.
I bring perennials
we're going to put
outside his window
in that little speck of earth
                    called 'the park'.
My father brightens up —
he plants and waters,
but can't grasp
for one thousand-splintered moment
that my parents are no longer alive.

Cry for Help

The bridge to yesterday is gone, my father
has no recollection of
our planting perennials in his flowerbed,
the flowers are nothing, a blank negative.
He is writing
        an (imaginary) letter,
for the bill's not right.
– Father, you've already
paid what's to be paid.
The sun is burning —
I call him on the phone to remind him
that the plants have to be watered.
His (dead) brother
            has gone down to the sea,
his (dead) sister is probably sitting now
in the breeze on a sandbank,
his (dead) mother
        has also gone,
he is totally alone...
– *One mustn't rob a person of*
                    their hope,
my father said when I was a child,
and we discussed
life lie or *ideal considerations.*
The sun is burning —
he also wants to go down to the shore,
his brother
    has been waiting for a long time.
Shall I obey this chaos?
Contribute
with a comforting lie?
My father is totally alone...
His voice grinds against
my eardrum,
a shrill snowfall sounds toweringly loud.

Handwriting

Dreamt that my father had a little window
up in the roof,
        the only window
he had to look out of.
In the room furniture stood stacked together
as in a lumber room.
The window was almost completely covered
by a large piece of cardboard,
           stormy grey.
In spite of this my father was trying
to squeeze his way
between cupboards, chests-of-drawers and a bureau
                             – – – standing on tiptoe
in order to look up through the last crack,
where a ray of light still
           penetrated.
He didn't complain, but I searched in consternation
for the nurses down long,
alarm-coloured linoleum corridors
with a sickly sweetish smell
           of overripe fruit.
There was also *another* problem:
My father's handwriting!
It was at vanishing-point —
or was he writing
        in ink made of snow?
The fact that I couldn't decipher the last remnants
of his writing
troubled me no less
than the view that was lacking.
I asked the nurses
to give my father his handwriting back.
The sought advice in the memory loss library,
but all the books were out on loan.
Moreover the key
to the box of pen and paper was
too short,
    hope was a thing of the past
they complained, looking up at the empty sky.

On the Opposite Coast

In no time my father's hair becomes
thin and white,
        the month of May
can be glimpsed through it,
the way the skin swiftly changes colour.
Patrol boats, rough swell,
heavy suitcases.
Memories from the war, when as a young man
my father fled with his mother
and his siblings,
drown out this moment.
A view of Øresund
and the Danish coast,
            far away, far away
and close to —
when he saw it from a hill
on a landowner's field
                in southern Sweden.
He used to work so early
that the morning sun struck the windows
of the outermost houses on the coast,
                    – one of which
was a landmark,
    his home,
where his father lived...
The windowpanes glowed along the Sound,
dream-sparks
crossed the water
            on cold, pain-clear days.
My father's hair
is thin and white,
            under the bones of his cranium
run veins that pulsate like rivers
from north to south —
the mind's Ice Age plants do not erode.

The Sky's Gravity

The sun sets, a momentary pain
                    tears at my father.
I sit down with him, take his hand,
familiar and unfamiliar
– haven't held it like this before.
His eyes roam
round the room, he asks
after books on my shelves:
                    Ekelöf, Ekman, Eliot,
looks out at the evening light in May,
comments on the clouds.
They crackle in a blue-white, open sky,
spread and disappear.
My father hold himself erect, his voice
pushes words between us,
                    a *mesh of language* —
so that reality
won't come too close,
just as bedtime stories
perhaps also once gave protection
from threatening danger:
                    enmity, savagery, malice?
I hold on to his hand,
                    time doesn't pass at all.
The sweat
breaks out on his temple.
His skin
is not the colour skin should be.
Suddenly his words can't find their way,
are just an inner echo,
but he is
        still my father.
In a mortal
chasm I listen
to his breathing, to falling
                    crystal rain,
a needle-like pricking in the darkness of the lungs.

My father is celebrating my birthday, though
he has no idea of it,
but he's on a visit —
and so one   doesn't pass out.

Winged Leap

Don't graze, just sit
with lowered head,
read with the lamp on
and an insect buzzing around.
My mother calls from the hospital.
Together
she and my father have waited
for circle-white hours.
A salt roar from an upright sea —
waves hack
at the shore, break in
over the threshold of consciousness
                         in a winged leap.
By turns my father rages
and brazenly flirts
with the young nurses.
The surf froths
and smokes. Out
             on a ledge of fear
he stares down.
Now it is not the war,
                but the body
that is the enemy.
I sink wide-awake
      and away —
drown on the bottom of myself,
                  fever-high.

My Brother's Eyes

– You're not going to kill me, are you?
says my father.
With my brother I wait
for my mother and sister
behind the shockwave's seconds.
My father sits in the chair of the crater,
                          stone cold.
I have lifted his feet up
on my knees
try with my hands
to rub them warm
under the threadbare hospital socks.
We look at each other,
                my ten years younger brother and I.
Bone-dry silence.
What is there to say to that question
that is boring its way
from misty atmospheres?
My father is dressed in the hospital's
chemical white clothes.
My brother's eyes
                are blue, blue.
And then filled with tears:
Total kidney failure combined
with more or less
total memory loss
                produces an astronomical sum
which does not offer the best prospects.
Should we follow my father's will
from a proud moment?
Avoid life-prolonging treatment?
– It's not difficult, says the doctor,
he's already decided for you…
Each year my father's fields bore new stones
fallen from the sky
or sprung up from the earth
                like flowers sown without plan.

We try to listen,
then decide to follow my father's wish
from long ago —
        but isn't that going to kill him?

Magic View

– Look, the water,
says my father, casting a gaze
out over the city's many red roofs.
I take his hand
         in mine,
he dozes, he wakes...
– Look, the snow,
says my father, looking out
on the last day of May.
I hold his hand
         tight,
he sleeps, he wakes...
– That's a big stretch of land,
says my father,
        who has had two farms
and now
keeps a lookout from his bed
on the hospital's 23rd floor.
In this slumbering body
          he will die.
Ice melts to fire —
I try to reach out to him
           on the last sandbank.

All the Celebrations

– WHY DO PEOPLE HAVE TO DIE?
my son says to me reproachfully.
– Life ought to last forever.
He has walked in the rain,
cried and cried
on the day
      he must say goodbye.
My father has come back
from the hospital.
He sits in his own clothes,
heroically erect
or quietly swaying,
eats at his writing desk
in the middle of the familiar room.
My father talks
      almost like someone risen from the dead —
about all the celebrations
in his life.
– And now, he says, here we all are again!

Next Stop Limbo

I dream that I'm driving
from Copenhagen
in the direction of Sweden.
I pass a figure
at high speed,
it's a motorway —
and I *can't*
    pull into the side.
I continue sleepwalker-like,
see in the rear mirror
        the darkness
sink around my father.
On the black asphalt
        in a parallel lane
I see him.
He stands in his light-coloured overcoat,
           waiting
at a bus stop
to be picked up by a bus
under a starless sky.
Apparently he has been waiting
from eternity and to eternity.
My heart closes up,
I watch in the mirror
        as the darkness swallows him behind me.
I leave my father behind,
      in the emptiness —
hurry onwards.
The coast opens out
      and ahead:
the tunnel, the bridge, the other shore...

Whose Hands?

Being is,
    that we are,
more we don't know.
We listen to my father's breathing,
try to read the slightest twitching of his face,
a wrinkle on the forehead, the quiver of an eyelid,
                        pain, not pain?
Outside, the world is in blossom.
In a rush of medication
my father raises
his arms before him – asks,
              whose hands are these?
I take hold of his hands.
– They're yours,
but now I'm holding them in mine.
Rest —
dive down under the surface again.
Sleep, wakening...
My father doesn't finish his sentences,
just sinks deeper into himself.
He doesn't hear the birds,
            but perhaps *something*
that has not been heard before?
He doesn't see the trees, can't
pick out the green river of light
outside the window, doesn't see
the bunch of flowers
my mother has picked for him.
But *something* in the air that we can't see,
               he sees —
something we don't perceive,
          he intercepts —
and the wild mushroom
my mother also found at the side of the ditch,
              that he can smell.
Its fragrance is recognised with a smile
as we hold it out:
        the sun, the cows, the grass in the meadow.

The night steals in on us, we speak
in muted voices.
When we smile at him
he smiles,
    – 'your' and 'my' are suspended.
We worry about our worry
for if we look worried,
he does too,
        – 'I' is identical with 'you'.
If my mother takes a bite of a piece of fruit
it is I or my sister
who get something to eat,
there is only one body in the room,
– and it is *ours*,
      a family body,
with a shared skin, shared nerves, shared veins,
all other grammar
     is superfluous.
My father looks at us, we look long at him,
are we islands of hope,
floating in the sea around him?
Hours fill and empty.
– Are you still here?
he asks, surprised,
as after long dozing he
opens his eyes —
      as though we might all be dead.

Good Night

My father is being dressed
in a nightshirt.
When I was a child
he sprinkled
stardust and moon gravel
down on my eyes,
When I was a child
I spoke as a child,
I understood as a child,
I thought as a child.
Every good night story
                    I received
had its own colour.
My father told them so a blind man
under the bell of darkness
would be able to see
                    a rainbow.
I slept and dreamt
the impossible
far away from the world's anxiety.
I turn around,
        turn towards him,
see in my father's eyes
stardust and moon gravel.
Now the night is coming —
                    the long night.
Milky ways of morphine
murmur
through his body
        with the light's heaviness
                    of pain's cessation.

At Least One Wound

– *The body always has at least one wound*,
my father said in front of the mirror,
where he was tying his tie,
when for the first time I saw
                              blood streaming
from my knee, which I had grazed.
– *The body always has at least one wound*
is the first whole sentence I remember
my father addressing to me,
in those days when I had just begun
to get to know the world.
I was four years old
and took part
              in my life's
first philosophical discussion:
– WHY DO WE HAVE TO DIE?
My father breathes the darkness
locked inside himself.
– *It hurts* —
is the last sentence my father
says to me
            on his deathbed.
After a whole day
without communication being possible
this sentence stands
clear
as a wound may shine.
The afternoon's silence exposes the words.
Look
how the wound is glowing.
– *It hurts* —
      but between these two sentences
a life has unfolded,
              holy, holy...
For as Theophanes, the Greek,
in Tarkovsky's *Andrei Rublev*,
after all kinds of trouble
                    blurts out:
– *It's so pretty, though, and now it's snowing.*

Double Spiral

The way down into the mountain
                        is narrow and steep,
I hear the water rushing
deep below me.
Draw
with the chalk,
so it crumbles under my fingernails,
a cascade of circles
on the wall of the cave,
                        whipcrack of double spirals
made of shadows that flicker
and smarting
contract.
The last pain
is the first thing
that meets the one who comes next...
Concentric time
the child
pierces a hole with its scream
and steps into the world
where we stole
            from love,
for we took it from others.
The night sky goes through me
and the light of tunnel mouths —
that morning,
shortly after the wolf-hour, where my father dies.

Flash

A kernel of nothing in a shell of everything,
the death-crystal
    of the naked moment.
The inner flash of silence
and above the greatest ocean the lyre of lightning —
a many-faceted gleam, the thunderous light
                      of a caress.

War and Peace

So it's *now* I must come,
it says on the telephone.
The first ring-tones are already
eating through the walls
to tell me the same thing.
Stars are falling. Of millions of years
it is this *now* —
the earliest morning hour,
                      acid-washed and transparent.
The chestnut tree in my street
has shed its flowers,
              a steaming bloodbath
of white and red before my feet.
My eyes
      go dark. Never more never.
I get into the car,
drive
into the kingdom of the mortal
along empty roads
              down into a cavern's blackness,
but only to Notice
that my father,
though he is still warm —
              IS no more...
Only to See, Hear and Smell
that my father
          IS no more...
Breaking morning, a rent
              in the mouldered garment.
Heart of ice, musculature of death, no retouching.
A body of fossilised wood
he has left behind. And a name
I must bear.
Yes —
there is a power cut affecting
              the whole globe.
– And perhaps that's why a candle stands lit in its holder.

Snow Bouquet

My father is taking
with him to the grave
                a white lilac
– a poem by Lars Norén,
                picked
for him by the nurses.
                ... I could not have found
a better bouquet
in any other garden.
Lilacs, snow —
        they chose for my father,
probably
without having read
one of my favourite books.
White lilac
        put there,
where the breathing stopped.
The damp smell of light
numbs the room,
silence floats.
I don't play
        with death —
for it is real.

Cold Morning

What for me is the present
is a future
    my father will not know.
Behind ear-splitting silence
his body has
        grown cold.
In my muscles
the cold feels
literally translated. Blue-black.
The morning rises
between the houses —
I move around
in a shadow realm
        of *no* father.
A dog's sudden barking
cleanses the heart.
Perhaps one day something
will knock
    and let itself in?

Dreamless Moment

Sky drowningly blue
above lizards and birds,
sun-white gravel
crunches beneath one's shoes.
Close to me I hold the urn
with my father's ashes —
                no different
from a child who is settling down.
The urn is heavy, it is *more*
than ashes and farewell,
                it is the swarm
                        of moments,
what I remember of my father;
what we all remember
                without being able to measure
either the days or the nights.
We carry the urn out to the grave,
I lower it
into a giddying
        depth
down to the teeming of the dead.
A mountain
sinks into the earth,
a wall falls, a shield is gone.
My tongue freezes...
Now there is *nothing*
                between me and death.
Like when every Wednesday the sirens
are tested
my head is filled
                with massively rushing silence —

The Flesh's Garb

That dress
I would have bought
if I'd been twenty years
                younger,
hangs in the window,
           dripping red
with light —
like an angel
      chained to a weapons dump.

Shadow Pulse

The birds' wedge of cries,
                    an open gate.
Come naked into
the world, go out
naked.
My father's corpse is gone,
                    burned and removed
from the earth's surface.
A pulse scratched into stone
and roads
      that branch away.
Death
we don't share —
but my father
is in my thoughts,
          as always,
still gets bills and letters sent to him.
The furniture is where it usually is,
the things
are still 'his':
the clothes (still with his smell),
the shoes (with the contour of his toes),
the cufflinks, the watch,
the books, the paper knife, the spectacles,
the box with the rose, the box with the rose.
When the drawers in the writing desk
are pulled out,
          they are full
of lost light.
The world remains,
          even after
my father has left it.
Ash writing. Ash days. Ash blossoming.
Resoundingly clear
          it is *there*.

Traceless Shoes

My father doesn't see the swallows in the air,
doesn't hear the young ones
                    mimicking
their parents' song.
My father won't smell the jasmine
placed like a frost-sparkling bouquet
on his table,
won't throw the door open on the raw scent of rain,
when earth and sky are blended,
                    won't stop short
at that metal fence
which separates inside from outside.
A man
with the same shoe size
as my father
wants his shoes.
Wonderful! Now these shoes will
                    go on walking,
to unfamiliar places —
they won't find
my father, won't
bring him back to life.
Each footstep will only
drag itself further and further
                    away.

Voice from the River

The mouth is open, the words
sleepless circles in the water:
The things I can neither
ask my father about
any more
nor please him with
spread waking
            echoes.
The arm he won't
put around my shoulder.
The gaze he won't
direct towards me.
The smell is gone,
the laughter.
The witness, the future witness.
Echo upon echo,
growing annual rings
of black-rimmed sorrow.
I have lost my father
to himself —
but a tree
        that falls
or is pulled up by its roots,
can give light unexpectedly strong.
                        Look!

Words Can't Be Buried

Beloved was my father,
　　　　　　and the first person in the world
to whom I gave a name —
　　　　　　in the form of a self-ignited
sound,
before I could utter the word
　　　　　　'father'.
It doesn't get lost,
doesn't vanish out
　　　　　of the language,
isn't on the list of threatened words,
can't be buried
　　　in forgetting.
The word 'father' exists,
but only as a concept
or multi-coloured memory.
An extinct species
can't swim, can't climb, can't fly —
just as my father
can't speak any more,
　　　　　　can't listen or call.
Ashes in an urn
　　　　　are not a father...
If I say
　　'father',
I can't wake him.
　　　　I live
in the word's shadow
– for *who* ever keeps what he promises?

The Hub of the Wheel

Round and round, the wheel
never returns
HOME —
the world in flames.
I am a movement
transmitted in writing.
What I say
are words
from the hub of the wheel.
From its depths
the case mysteriously over-
                    flows,
floats as stones
on the sea
of my father's fields. Circles
spread out,
penetrating.
Eyes, ears,
the heart's hammering pulse.
There is plenty of room
for six billion or more
lonely people
to look up
        without drowning
in the blackly undulating, wide-open night.

Words Burn on the Tongue

Before the serpent's pain-bite
Eurydice's longing:
People
should wake people,
        caress
one another a little more.
Let the heart flame up
in the darkness,
let sorrow turn
        to relief.
There is nothing between us
but everything.
There must be
a possible escape route
for flying birds
        in the blood —
a rose rain, a soughing
        so clear
that on nights
        when no one is sleeping
it can be heard by a stubborn star.

The Endless of Halls of Memory

I can't feel the brain,
                although it's mine,
can't sense it like my heart, my sex.
The brain is silent
as no other organ in the body
is silent,
    but always awake.
With the hands
I grasp,
    it can be felt.
With the brain
I grasp,
    it can't be felt
even though the brain is encamped
                        in my skull,
only in the soul
            is a shower of gashes deposited.
Curiosity drives me,
it has roots in the brain,
                I live
in the fever of language, try to understand
why the brain
            is magic.
Why it not only
contains a life's images,
but also remembers
            millennially.
To remember is *not* to forget —
but forgetting
        is blind
to the possibility of being able to remember.
Forgetting wipes the slate clean,
it isn't just a gift of mercy,
but also a misfortune,
a reality... The enigmatic.

OUTRO

Tarkovsky's Horses

In that beauty a horse
displays,
standing in sun
on a grassy field,
which I'm travelling past in a train,
a few days after
my father died —
          I suddenly see him again.
The passage of
          the greenness...
With the same exalted peace
Tarkovsky's horses
in *Andrei Rublev*
          radiate
in the film's final images,
my father is present,
resting in himself.
He has been shrouded
in flames,
   and I have carried
his urn to the burial place.
Being is not
being
without pain.
I carry him
within me
like a new authority.
The tongue's power —
          Eurydice is singing.
Something in the horse's essence
makes him emerge.
A shadow shines,
          now he simply IS here.